Come Back, Pip!

Story by Jan Weeks

Illustrations by Claire Bridge

Mrs. Sands lived next door
to Ben and his family.

One day,
Mrs. Sands had to go away for a week.
She asked Ben and his mother
to take care of her canary.

The canary was called Pip.

"Please take good care of Pip,"
said Mrs. Sands, as she put the cage
and birdseed on the table.
"I love him very much."

"We will put the cage up high,"
said Mom.

"And I'll put the cat outside
when I feed Pip," said Ben.

One morning,
when Ben went to look at Pip,
the cage was empty!
Pip was gone!

"I must have left the cage door open
when I fed him last night," said Ben.
He felt very bad about it.
What would Mrs. Sands say?

Ben started to look for Pip.
First he looked
all around the kitchen,
but Pip was nowhere to be seen.

Ben ran to look in the other rooms.
"I hope Pip is still inside,"
he said to himself.
"I will have to find him."

Ben looked **behind** things
and **under** things
and on **top** of things.

He still couldn't find Pip anywhere.

Then he saw the cat.
She was sitting on a chair,
licking her paws.

"Oh, no!" said Ben, to Socks the cat.
"You must have eaten Pip.
You bad, **bad** cat!
Mrs. Sands will be so upset."
Ben was nearly crying.

Just then,
Ben heard a whistle.

"I think that could be Pip,"
he said.
"I wonder where he is?"

Then Ben heard another whistle,
and another.

The whistles were coming
from the bathroom.

There was Pip.
He was sitting by the window
in the sun.

"The cat **didn't** eat you after all!"
said Ben.
He shut the bathroom door,
and ran to get the cage.
He put some more birdseed in it.

Pip was still by the window
when Ben came back.

He put the cage down,
and hid just outside the door
to watch.

Pip was hungry. He flew down,
and hopped into the cage.

Ben crept over and shut the little door.
He was **very** glad
that Pip was safe
inside the cage again.